Super-Smart Shopping

An introduction to financial literacy

by Mattie Reynolds

RED
CHAIR
•PRESS•

Please visit our website at **www.redchairpress.com**.

Find a free catalog of all our high-quality products for young readers.

Super-Smart Shopping

Publisher's Cataloging-In-Publication Data
(Prepared by The Donohue Group, Inc.)

Reynolds, Mattie.
Super-smart shopping : an introduction to financial literacy / by Mattie Reynolds.
p. : col. ill. ; cm. -- (Start smart: money)
Issued also as an ebook.
Summary: Before spending money, smart shoppers save, budget, and compare. This book will teach you words and ideas about spending.
Interest age group: 004-008.
Includes bibliographical references and index.
ISBN: 978-1-937529-43-7 (hardcover)
ISBN: 978-1-937529-39-0 (pbk.)
1. Shopping--Juvenile literature. 2. Consumer education--Juvenile literature. 3. Children--Finance, Personal--Juvenile literature. 4. Shopping. 5. Consumer education. 6. Finance, Personal. I. Title. II. Title: Super smart shopping
TX335.5 .R49 2013
640.73   2012943328

Photo credits:
Dreamstime: pages front cover, 1, 7, 8, 14, 15, 20
iStockphoto LP: pages 6
Shutterstock Images LLC: 3, 4, 5, 9, 10, 11, 12, 13, 17, 18, 19, 21, back cover

Reading specialist: Linda Cornwell, Literacy Connections Consulting

This edition first published in 2013 by

Red Chair Press LLC   PO Box 333   South Egremont, MA 01258-0333

Printed in The United States of America

1 2 3 4 5 17 16 15 14 13

Table of Contents

Words in **bold type** are defined in the glossary.

CHAPTER 1

Why People Buy Things

People buy things for many reasons. A person may buy something they need such as food. A person may also buy something they want like a new backpack. Sometimes **shopping** can be a fun activity.

But a smart shopper knows that spending money to buy things is not a game. Smart shoppers think about the cost of every item before buying.

Smart shoppers think about the cost of items.

Many adults work and earn money. Families
use money to buy things they need and want.
Families need a place to live. They need electricity
for their home. And they may want furniture for
the home.

Before buying a home, some people make a **budget**. A budget lets a family know how much money they can spend. The family may need a house or apartment with two bedrooms, but they may want four bedrooms. A budget helps them know what they can afford.

Smart shoppers know how much money they can spend for things they need and want before they buy.

Saving, or putting money aside, is a smart way to plan for buying things later. If a family buys a home, they may want to shop for new tables or chairs. If the family saves $50 each month for a new sofa, they will have $200 after four months.

By going to different stores, the family can **compare** the cost of items. One store sells a sofa for $180. Another store sells a sofa for $200. The difference is $20. A smart shopper thinks about what is important to them before buying. The money saved could be used to buy something else the family wants.

CHAPTER 2

Making Good Choices

A family has many things to buy. Families buy food and clothes. Some people make a list of what to buy before they go shopping. Making a list is one way to spend wisely. By buying items only on the list, smart shoppers will not spend money for things they do not need.

Kids can help their family make wise choices when shopping, too. Before shopping, know how much money can be spent. Make a list of items to buy. And shop for what the family needs before buying what someone wants.

Some people make a list before shopping.

Ella's mother shops for her family's food each week. She makes a list of things she needs to buy. But it is easy to buy items she does not have on her list. When Ella goes shopping with her mother, Ella marks items off the list as they shop. Now they buy only what they need.

Trudy and her parents go to the market to buy food and other items. Trudy helps compare different items. She looks at the cost of each item. She also compares the size or number of servings for each item. One box of cereal has 20 servings and another has 30 servings. A super-smart shopper looks at both price and size.

Maya has been saving her **allowance** for weeks. She wants to buy a new sweatshirt. Maya knows she must compare prices. But Maya is a smart shopper and knows to compare other features too. She asks herself, "Will this sweatshirt be warm enough? Does the color go with my favorite shoes?" Maya wants to spend her money wisely.

Sam wants a new glove before baseball season starts in June. The glove is **expensive** and Sam's old glove is good. Sam wants the new glove, but he does not need it to play now. In August, Sam has saved enough money for the new glove. Sam decides to wait until baseball season is over. He knows that the new glove will go on sale. Then he can buy the new glove for less money.

CHAPTER 3

How People Shop

When someone is ready to buy things, there are many different ways to shop. A person can go to a store to look for an item. Some people shop by looking at catalogs or magazines. Many people shop by visiting online stores. How do you know which is the best way to shop for what you need?

Before shopping, decide how quickly the item is needed. Some foods should be bought in a store. But clothes, toys, or other goods may be bought in other ways. They may not be needed so quickly. However a person shops, smart shoppers remember to compare items.

Smart shoppers compare items in a store.

In a store, shoppers may find several types
of an item. Smart shoppers can compare
one item to another.

Many smart shoppers know the prices and features of goods found in other stores. They may make a list. Catalogs and online searches help an adult shop wisely. Then the smart shopper can compare items in a store with items found in other places.

Libby's aunt Tia shops on her computer. Online shopping can be a good way for adults to find items not found easily in stores. Before Tia shops online, she searches for places that sell the item she wants to buy.

Super-smart shoppers know they should compare items before buying. In a store, a shopper may be able to compare items easily. In a catalog or online store, it may be more difficult to compare one item to another. It takes more time to shop wisely.

Glossary

allowance: money paid regularly to a child for specific purposes or tasks

budget: an estimate of income, or money earned, and expenses for a period of time

compare: to note what is the same and different between two or more things

expensive: costing a lot of money

shopping: to look in a store or place to buy goods

For More Information

Books

Firestone, Mary. *Spending Money* (Learning About Money). Mankato, MN: Capstone Press, 2005.

Larson, Jennifer S. *Do I Need It? Or Do I Want It?* (Lightning Bolt Books). Minneapolis, MN: Lerner Publishing, 2010.

Otfinoski, Steve. *The Kid's Guide to Money: Earning It, Saving It, Spending It, Growing It, Sharing It.* New York, NY: Scholastic, 1995.

Web Sites

Practical Money Skills for Life
http://www.practicalmoneyskills.com/games/

TheMint.org: Spending
http://www.themint.org/kids/spending.html

Note to educators and parents: Our editors have carefully reviewed these web sites to ensure they are suitable for children. Web sites change frequently, however, and we cannot guarantee that a site's future contents will continue to meet our high standards of quality and educational value. You may wish to preview these sites and closely supervise children whenever they access the Internet.

Index

About the Author

Mattie Reynolds practices the four basic skills of financial literacy in her life. She earned money in the insurance business and learned to save for things her family needed. Mattie continues to be a smart shopper buying what she needs and saving for what she wants. She shares with her church and charity in Duncan, Oklahoma, where she lives.